First World War
and Army of Occupation
War Diary
France, Belgium and Germany

46 DIVISION
Divisional Troops
B Squadron Yorkshire Hussars
26 February 1915 - 31 May 1916

WO95/2673/1

The Naval & Military Press Ltd
www.nmarchive.com
Published in association with The National Archives

Published by

The Naval & Military Press Ltd

Unit 10 Ridgewood Industrial Park,

Uckfield, East Sussex,

TN22 5QE England

Tel: +44 (0) 1825 749494

www.naval-military-press.com

www.nmarchive.com

This diary has been reprinted in facsimile from the original. Any imperfections are inevitably reproduced and the quality may fall short of modern type and cartographic standards.

© **Crown Copyright**
Images reproduced by permission of The National Archives, London, England, 2015.

Contents

Document type	Place/Title	Date From	Date To
Heading	WO95/2673/1		
Heading	46th Division Divl Troops 'B' Soon A.P.W.O. Yorks. Hussars Feb 1915-May 1916 To 17 Corps.		
Heading	46 B Sqd Yorks Hussars Vol XIV		
Heading	46 B Sqd Yorks Hussars Vol XIII		
Heading	War Diary of "B" Squadron A.P.W.O. Yorkshire Hussars. from February 26th 1915 to March 31st 1915 Volume I		
War Diary	Harlow	26/02/1915	26/02/1915
War Diary	Southampton	27/02/1915	27/02/1915
War Diary	Le Havre	28/02/1915	28/02/1915
War Diary	Cassell	29/02/1915	09/03/1915
War Diary	Pradelles.	11/03/1915	11/03/1915
War Diary	Estaires.	16/03/1915	16/03/1915
War Diary	Merris	17/03/1915	17/03/1915
War Diary	Ootersteene	20/03/1915	20/03/1915
War Diary	Armentiers	25/03/1915	25/03/1915
War Diary	Ootersteene	26/03/1915	26/03/1915
War Diary	Nieppe	31/03/1915	31/03/1915
Heading	46th Division. B. Squadron Yorkshire Hussars (Divl Cavy 46th (NM) Div) Vol II 1-30.4.15		
War Diary	Ootersteene.	01/04/1915	16/04/1915
War Diary	Bailleul-St Jans Cappell	16/04/1915	22/04/1915
Heading	46th Division. "B" Squad Yorkshire Hussars Vol III 2-31.5.15		
War Diary	Bailleul-St Jans Cappel	02/05/1915	31/05/1915
Heading	46th Division. "B" Squadn Yorkshire Hussars (46th Divl Cavy:) Vol IV 1-30.6.15		
War Diary	Bailleul	01/06/1915	21/06/1915
War Diary	St Jans Cappell	21/06/1915	22/06/1915
War Diary	Westoutre	23/06/1915	30/06/1915
War Diary	Wolvergham	11/06/1915	11/06/1915
Heading	46th Division. B. Squadn Yorkshire Hussars (Divl Cav. 46th Divl) Vol V From 1st to 28th July 1915		
War Diary	In Camp W. of Westoutre Poperinghe	01/07/1915	28/07/1915
War Diary		08/07/1915	08/07/1915
Heading	46th Division. B. Squad Yorkshire Hussars (46th Divl Coy) Vol VI Aug 1.15		
War Diary	Elhoek Farm N. Of Abeele Poperinghe Rd (Ref Belgium Sheet 27. L15B 8.2)	01/08/1915	31/08/1915
Heading	46th Division "B" Squadron Yorkshire Hussars (46th Divl Cavalry) Vol VII Sept 15		
War Diary	N Of Abeele Poperinghe Road.	01/09/1915	16/09/1915
War Diary	Wippenhoek (Sheet 27. NE) 1/20,000 L 34. C	17/09/1915	30/09/1915
Heading	46th Division "B" Sqn. Yorkshire Gds. Oct 1915 Vol VIII		
War Diary	Wippenhoek Farm. Poperinghe-Boeschepe Rd.	01/10/1915	01/10/1915
War Diary	Vieux Berquin	02/10/1915	02/10/1915
War Diary	Busnes	03/10/1915	05/10/1915
War Diary	Fontenelle Farm	06/10/1915	06/10/1915

War Diary	Bethune	07/10/1915	31/10/1915
War Diary		13/10/1915	27/10/1915
Heading	46th Division. "B" Sqd. Yorks Hussars. Nov Vol IX		
War Diary	Bethune (Bethune 1/40,000 L5.B.5.4)	01/11/1915	05/11/1915
War Diary	Bethune (Bethune 1/40,000 L5.B.5.4)	02/11/1915	21/11/1915
War Diary	Paradis	22/11/1915	30/11/1915
Heading	46th Div. 'B' Sqdn. Yorkshire Hrs. Dec Vol X		
War Diary	Paradis.	01/12/1915	04/12/1915
War Diary	La Haye	05/12/1915	13/12/1915
War Diary	Mont De Lambres	19/12/1915	31/12/1915
Heading	B Sqd Yorkshire Hrs Jan Vol XI		
War Diary	Mont De Lambres	01/01/1916	10/01/1916
War Diary	In The Train	11/01/1916	13/01/1916
War Diary	Camp La Valentine Marseille.	13/01/1916	26/01/1916
War Diary	In The Train	26/01/1916	29/01/1916
War Diary	Famechon	30/01/1916	31/01/1916
War Diary	Famechon	01/02/1916	11/02/1916
War Diary	Domqueur	11/02/1916	18/02/1916
War Diary	Mont Plaisir	18/02/1916	24/02/1916
War Diary	Canaples	24/02/1916	29/02/1916
War Diary	Candas	29/02/1916	05/03/1916
War Diary	Sibiville	06/03/1916	08/03/1916
War Diary	Gouy En Ternois	09/03/1916	10/03/1916
War Diary	Aubigny	11/03/1916	11/03/1916
War Diary	Bethonsart	12/03/1916	21/04/1916
War Diary	Ternas.	22/04/1916	07/05/1916
War Diary	Gouy En Ternois.	08/05/1916	31/05/1916

WO95/26731

46TH DIVISION
DIVL TROOPS

'B' SQDN A.P.W.O. YORKS. HUSSARS

FEB 1915 - MAY 1916

To 17 Corps

46

B Sqd York Hussars

Vol XIV

46

"B" Sqd York Hussars
Vol XIII

46/
1/1 North Midland Division

13/4/39.

CONFIDENTIAL

WAR DIARY.

of

"B" Squadron. A.P.W.O. Yorkshire Hussars.

from FEBRUARY 26th 1915 to MARCH 31st 1915.

VOLUME I

Army Form C. 2118.

WAR DIARY
or
INTELLIGENCE SUMMARY
(Erase heading not required.)

Instructions regarding War Diaries and Intelligence Summaries are contained in F. S. Regs., Part II. and the Staff Manual respectively. Title pages will be prepared in manuscript.

Hour, Date, Place			Summary of Events and Information	Remarks and references to Appendices
5.15 A.M.	26.2.15	HARLOW.	Entrained for SOUTHAMPTON. "B" Squadron, Yorkshire Hussars less 50 men.	
12 Noon	26.2.15	"	Remainder of Squadron left.	
5. P.M.	27.2.15	SOUTHAMPTON	Embarked.	
9. A.M.	28.2.15	LE HAVRE.	Disembarked and proceeded at 9. P.M. up country.	
6. P.M.	29.2.15	CASSELL	Arrived and were billeted at LES TROIS ROIS.	
8.15.	9.3.15	"	Marched to PRADELLES and billeted.	
11. A.M.	11.3.15	PRADELLES.	Marched to ESTAIRES and billeted RUE CUL DU SAC.	
9.3. A.M.	16.3.15	ESTAIRES.	Marched to MERRIS. billeted	
—	17	MERRIS.	Headquarters moved to OOTERSTEENE. Inspected by Field Marshal Sir John French.	

1247 W 3299 200,000 (E) 8/14 J.B.C. & A. Forms/C. 2118/11.

Army Form C. 2118.

WAR DIARY
or
INTELLIGENCE SUMMARY
(Erase heading not required.)

Hour, Date, Place	Summary of Events and Information	Remarks and references to Appendices
9.A.M. 20.3.15 OOTERSTEENE.	3 Officers and 60 men marched to ARMENTIERS for instruction in the trenches.	
12 NOON 25.3.15 ARMENTIERS.	Above ½ Squadron returned to billets at OOTERSTEENE.	
2.P.M. 26.3.15 OOTERSTEENE.	Remaining ½ Squadron (3 Officers and 60 men) marched to NIEPPE and were attached to XIX Hussars "A" Sqdn. with 4th Inf. Div: for Trench instruction.	
10.A.M. 31.3.15 NIEPPE.	This ½ Squadron returned to Billets at OOTERSTEENE.	

121/5320

46th Division.

B. Squadron Yorkshire Hussars
(Div¹ Cav⁰y. 46th (NM) Div⁴)

Vol III 1 – 30.4.15

Army Form C. 2118.

WAR DIARY
or
INTELLIGENCE SUMMARY
(Erase heading not required.)

Instructions regarding War Diaries and Intelligence Summaries are contained in F. S. Regs., Part II. and the Staff Manual respectively. Title pages will be prepared in manuscript.

Hour, Date, Place	Summary of Events and Information	Remarks and references to Appendices
1.4.15 to 5.4.15 OOTERSTEENE.	Squadron continued ordinary Routine Training (Bayonet Fighting, Equitation, Mounted & Dismounted Attack in Woods & against Farms, Advance Guards.	
5.4.15 do	Attached temporarily to 4th Cavalry Brigade for Training.	
11 a.m. 6.4.15 do	Squadron Paraded and proceeded to new Billets at ST JANS CAPPELL, on arrival there found there was no accommodation so returned to old Billets at OOTERSTEENE.	
7.4.15 to 12.4.15 do.	Continued Squadron training.	
13.4.15 to 15.4.15 do	do do also 2 Officers & 20 Men instructed in Demolition & Bomb throwing.	
2.30 p.m. 16.4.15 do	Paraded 2.30 p.m. and marched to new Billets Div. area at ST JANS CAPPELL.	
16.4.15 to 30.4.15. BAILLEUL - ST JANS CAPPELL	Billeted. One Ride from BAILLEUL to BAILLEUL - ST JANS CAPPELL Road.	
9.50 p.m. 22.4.15 do.	Squadron received orders from Headquarters, N.M.D. to "Stand to" and be Prepared to move at short notice owing to attack on Canadian Division.	

D

1247 W 3299 200,000 (E) 8/14 J.B.C. & A. Forms/C. 2118/11.

181/5610

46th Division

"B" Squad" Yorkshire Hussars

Vol III — 2 — 31. 5. 15.

Army Form C. 2118.

WAR DIARY
INTELLIGENCE SUMMARY
(Erase heading not required.)

Hour, Date, Place	Summary of Events and Information	Remarks and references to Appendices
6 P.M. 2.5.15. BAILLEUL – ST JANS CAPEL.	2 Officers & 60 O.R. marched for night-digging under orders of S/Staff: Inf: Brigade.	
4.5.15 do:	1 Officer & 50 O.R. billeted at ALDERSHOT CAMP for 4 days' digging under orders of Staff: Inf: Brigade.	
8.5.15 do:	Each night 1 Officer & 30 O.R. performed the duties of night-patrolling for the N.M. Div., viz: patrols for protection of Telephone & Telegraph wires & anti-sniper patrols.	
8.5.15 10.5.15 do:		
12.5.15 31.5.15 do:	4 days in each week 1 Officer & 50 O.R. proceeded as a digging party to WOLVERGHEM & neighbourhood under orders of Staff: Inf: Brigade. 5 A.M. – 12.30 P.M.	

Shanno Burton
Lieut:
for O.C. B Sq:
Yorkshire Hussars.

121/6034

46th Division

"B" Squad: Yorkshire Hussars (46th Div: Cav:)

Vol IV 1 — 30.6.15.

46th Division

Army Form C. 2118.

WAR DIARY
or
INTELLIGENCE SUMMARY
(Erase heading not required.)

Instructions regarding War Diaries and Intelligence Summaries are contained in F. S. Regs., Part II. and the Staff Manual respectively. Title pages will be prepared in manuscript.

Hour, Date, Place	Summary of Events and Information	Remarks and references to Appendices
1.6.15 BAILLEUL	4 days in each week 1 Officer & 50 O.R's proceeded as a digging party to WOLVERGHEM or neighbourhood under orders of Staffs. Inf. Brigade. 5 A.M. to 12·30 P.M.	
to		
21.6.15. ST JANS CAPPEL	The 3 remaining days were employed in Squadron training, Equitation and cleaning up.	11th June horse issued.
22.6.15 do	Squadron handed 12 midnight to change Billets and marched to new Billets in WEST of WESTOUTRE – POPERINGHE Road. (Ref. BELGIUM. Sheet 28. G 32. A.6.1.)	
23.6.15 WESTOUTRE	Building and arranging Camp.	
25.6.15 do		
26.6.15 do	Leave opened for N.C.O's men of the Squadron. 20 proceeded to ENGLAND on this day.	
26.6.15 do	Squadron employed in Routine training (Equitation	
to 30.6.15 do	Route Reconnaissance)	
11.6.15. WOLVERGHEM	2063 pte harsh wounded.	

1247 W 3299 200,000 (E) 8/14 J.B.C. & A. Forms/C. 2118/11.

46th Division

95/9/12

B. Squadron Yorkshire Hussars
(Div: Cav: 46th Div:)

Vol V
From 1st to 28th July 1915

Army Form C. 2118.

WAR DIARY
or
INTELLIGENCE SUMMARY
(Erase heading not required.)

Hour, Date, Place	Summary of Events and Information	Remarks and references to Appendices
1.7.15 In Camp. W. of WESTOUTRE	For 5 days in each week during this period the Squadron furnished a party of 1 Officer and 50 Other Ranks for Digging. Working in	
28.7.15 POPERINGHE Rd.	Winning as follows:- July 1st – 9th at ZILLEBECKE. 11th – 31st at KRUISSTRAAT.	
28.7.15 do	The 2 remaining days in each week were filled by Ordinary Squadron Training Routine. The Squadron moved at 3. A.M. to change Billets, moving to SCHOUDEMONTHOEK FARM. (Ref. BELGIUM. Sheet 27. L. 15.B.8.1.)	
8.7.15	Leave was granted to the Squadron at the rate of 5 per day from July 1st to 7th, from July 8th to 16th one each day, from July 18th to 30th one every other day. 2485 Pte Robson. C.J. wounded.	

Digby Lawsir. Capt.
For O.C. B.S. Squadron
Yorkshire Dragoons.
D.

121/6753

46th Division

B. Speed: Lt Col hus Hussard (46th Div Cav)
Vol VII
August 1. 15

Army Form C. 2118.

WAR DIARY
or
INTELLIGENCE SUMMARY
(Erase heading not required.)

Instructions regarding War Diaries and Intelligence Summaries are contained in F. S. Regs, Part II. and the Staff Manual respectively. Title pages will be prepared in manuscript.

Hour, Date, Place	Summary of Events and Information	Remarks and references to Appendices
1. 8. 15. ELHOEK FARM.	Squadron Routine. Parades in Camp.	
2. 8. 15 N. OF ABEELE -	Squadron found party of 1 Officer + 52 men for work on BRIDGE. 14.	
3. 8. 15 POPERINGHE Rd. (Ref BELGIUM Sheet 27. L. 15. B. 8. 2.)		
4. 8. 15 to 8. 8. 15	Squadron found party of 1 Officer + 25 N.C.O.s then for work in YPRES.	
9. 8. 15 to 11. 8. 15	Squadron training + ordinary Routine in Camp.	
12. 8. 15	Squadron found 1 Officer + 25 N.C.O.s then for work in YPRES.	
13. 8. 15 14. 8. 15	Squadron training + Camp Routine.	
14. 8. 15	2 Lieut. A Gpt proceeded to ENGLAND on one month leave under Army Act 252/1915.	
15. 8. 15 to 18. 8. 15	Squadron found party of 1 Officer + 50 N.C.O.s then for fortification work at KRUISSTRAAT.	
17. 8. 15	Squadron Routine. Training in Camp.	
20. 8. 15 21. 8. 15 22. 8. 15	Squadron found party of 1 Officer + 50 N.C.O.s then for fortification work at KRUISSTRAAT.	
23. 8. 15 to 29. 8. 15	Squadron found party of 1 Officer + 27 N.C.O.s then for making new dug-outs at KRUISSTRAAT.	
30. 8. 15	Squadron found party of 1 Officer + 27 N.C.O.s then who proceeded to the Trenches for the day for repair work in ZILLEBEKE SWITCH.	
31. 8. 15		

Army Form C. 2118.

WAR DIARY
or
INTELLIGENCE SUMMARY
(Erase heading not required.)

Hour, Date, Place	Summary of Events and Information	Remarks and references to Appendices
31.8.15 ELHOEK FARM N.of. ABEELE – POPERINGHE Rd. (Ref. BELGIUM Sheet 27 L.15.B.8.2)	Owing to unpracticability and mud of trenches in getting up to the trenches & back a diminished party of men for this work was detailed to remain in the trenches in 3 days relief.	
31.8.15	1 Sergt + 1 man proceeded on Ordnance leave to ENGLAND under Army Order 252/1915.	
10.30 pm 31.8.15	Lieut R.S. Dodson was killed in action in the trenches here by 8" Bats thrown at Forester's, with whom he was undergoing a course of instruction.	

Digby Lawson Capt.
for O.C. "B" Squadron
Yorkshire Hussars.

46th Division

121/7018

"B" Squadron Jodhpur Hattlal
(46th Divl Cavalry)

Vol. VII

Sept 15

Army Form C. 2118.

WAR DIARY
or
INTELLIGENCE SUMMARY
(Erase heading not required.)

Instructions regarding War Diaries and Intelligence Summaries are contained in F.S. Regs., Part II. and the Staff Manual respectively. Title pages will be prepared in manuscript.

Hour, Date, Place	Summary of Events and Information	Remarks and references to Appendices
1.9.15 N of ABEELE —	The Squadron were engaged in rehearsing & reconnoitring Trenches in ZILLEBEKE SWITCH.	
to 9.9.15 POPERINGHE ROAD.	A party of 1 Officer, 1 Sergt & 20 men remaining up in Relief of 3 days.	
17.9.15 WIPPENHOEK (Sheet 27. N.E.	The Squadron changed Billets to farm at WIPPENHOEK Sheet 27. N.E. 20,000/1 L.34.C.	
18.9.15 20,000/1 L.34.C.		
19.9.15 "	Arranging Camp.	
20.9.15 "	A party of 1 Officer, 1 Sergt & 20 men remained at ZILLEBEKE SWITCH repairing Trenches etc.	
22.9.15 "	Squadron worked on fatigues in Camp, preparing Barns for Winter accommodation for the men & standings for the Horses.	
23.9.15 "		
26.9.15 "	Squadron commenced Regular Cavalry training and were practising Advanced Guard, Reconnaissance & patrols.	
27.9.15 "		
29.9.15 "	Orders received to be prepared to move at end of week.	
30.9.15 "		
	16/9/15 { Sergt Bay Rm J. 2/15 { 63½C Horse. } Proceed on one months leave under Army Res 10.9.15 Pte Brown. 7. } 252/1915	

Digby Lawson Capt.
for O.C. B Squadron
Yorkshire Dragoons

121/7599

46th Division

"B" Sqn. Yorkshire Yeo.

Oct 15

1 & VIII

Army Form C. 2118.

WAR DIARY
or
INTELLIGENCE SUMMARY
(Erase heading not required.)

Instructions regarding War Diaries and Intelligence Summaries are contained in F.S. Regs., Part II. and the Staff Manual respectively. Title pages will be prepared in manuscript.

Hour, Date, Place	Summary of Events and Information	Remarks and references to Appendices
1. X. 15. WIPPENHOEK FARM - POPERINGHE - BOESCHEPE Rd.	Warned to move with Division to new area.	
2. X. 15. VIEUX BERQUIN.	Squadron marched out from above Billet at 5 P.M. arriving VIEUX BERQUIN at 10.30 p.m.	
3. X. 15. BUSNES.	Squadron marched out above Billet at 6.15 p.m. arrived BUSNES. 10 p.m.	
4. X. 15. "	Worked at Billet, cleaning billets etc. and got all horses under cover.	
5. X. 15. "	2nd Lieut J. Anwill arrived this day vice Lieut E.L. Tudor Rodwell and was taken on strength of squadron.	
6 a.m. 6. X. 15 FONTENELLE FARM	Orders arrived to move. Squadron marched out at 10 a.m. and proceeded to FONTENELLE FARM (BETHUNE 40,000 E.7.C.) which was occupied by A.S.C. 2nd Div. and may to make in Billeting area. Squadron bivouaced for night in field adjoining.	
7. X. 15 BETHUNE	Billets having been found the Squadron in BETHUNE marched out from bivouac at 2 p.m. and arrived BETHUNE. 4.30 p.m. Officers billets: 21 Rue Michelet. Mens Billet: Clock Factory, Faubourg de Arras. Orderly Room: 177 Faubourg de Arras. Horse lines (Ordinary Squadron Routine	
8. X. 15. "		
10. X. 15. "		
11. X. 15. "		
12. X. 15. "	Issue party of 1 Officer + 40 N.C.O's + men to VERMELLES for improving trenches in WEST BOYAU. Horse lines changed to field just outside Clock Factory yard.	

Army Form C. 2118.

WAR DIARY
or
INTELLIGENCE SUMMARY
(Erase heading not required.)

Instructions regarding War Diaries and Intelligence Summaries are contained in F.S. Regs., Part II. and the Staff Manual respectively. Title pages will be prepared in manuscript.

Hour, Date, Place	Summary of Events and Information	Remarks and references to Appendices
12. X. 15 BETHUNE.	A party of 1 Officer + 50 N.C.O.s then proceeded to VERMELLES to fill water carts for Infantry in trenches.	
13. X. 15	Squadron paraded at 10.30 a.m. and proceeded to Horse lines at (BETHUNE 40,000 L.S.B.5.4.) where the Squadron proceeded dismounted to VERMELLES for duty as escort for Prisoners, taking water Bombs up to Front line trenches, and acting as Stretcher Bearers to wounded on return journey.	
14. X. 15	13/14th date of attack by 46th Div. on FOSSE. 8, the Squadron were employed on above duties all through the night, returning to Billets at 1 p.m. on the 14th. Supplies salvage party under G.O.C. 3rd Guards Brigade working from VERMELLES.	
15. X. 15	Squadron Routine.	
16. X. 15	Squadron supplied salvage party to work under G.O.C. 3rd Guards Bgde. working from VERMELLES.	
17. X. 15	1 N.C.O. + 7 men arrived as Reinforcement.	
18. X. 15	Squadron Routine.	
19. X. 15		
20. X. 15	Squadron paraded at 10.30 a.m. Full marching Order and proceeded to GOSNAY where they were inspected by G.O.C. 46th Division.	
21. X. 15		
22. X. 15 to 25. X. 15	Squadron worked under Troop arrangements. Trained in Musketry, Reconnaissance + Advance Guards.	

Army Form C. 2118.

WAR DIARY
or
INTELLIGENCE SUMMARY

(Erase heading not required.)

Instructions regarding War Diaries and Intelligence Summaries are contained in F. S. Regs., Part II. and the Staff Manual respectively. Title pages will be prepared in manuscript.

Hour, Date, Place	Summary of Events and Information	Remarks and references to Appendices
26. X. 15 BETHUNE	Commenced Horse Standings & Division gave permission to remain in BETHUNE.	
27. X. 15 to 30. X. 15 .	Horse Lines into yard of block Factory. Officers Billet changed to 15 Rue Eugene Shuyaert. Squadron worked as General Fatigue on Construction of Horse Standings.	
31. X. 15 .	Church Parade. No fatigues, by order of G.O.C. day to be observed as rest.	
13. X. 15 .	L/Cpl Kirby L — L/Cpl Brook G. wounded.	
25. X. 15 .	Sergt Poskitt A. L. Pte Precious G. Proceeded on Orchard Leave granted under Army Act 252/1915.	
27. X. 15 .	Pte Wilkinson J. S.	

Digby Lawson . Capt.

for O.C. B Squadron.
Yorkshire Hussars.

16th Hussars

"B" Sqn. 16th Hussars.
Nov.
Vol IX

12/44
15

WAR DIARY
or
INTELLIGENCE SUMMARY

(Erase heading not required.)

Army Form C. 2118.

Instructions regarding War Diaries and Intelligence Summaries are contained in F. S. Regs., Part II. and the Staff Manual respectively. Title pages will be prepared in manuscript.

Hour, Date, Place	Summary of Events and Information	Remarks and references to Appendices
1. XI. 15 to 4. XI. 15 BETHUNE (BETHUNE 1/40,000)	The Squadron worked at Horse Standings on General Fatigue.	
5. XI. 15 L.S.B.S.4		
2. XI. 15 "	A F.G.C.M. met at Squadron Office at 10 a.m. to try No. 2342 Pte Birtwhistle J.D. accused of stealing a watch, the property of the Comet was Guilty and sentenced to 3 months F.P. No. 1.	
3. XI. 15	Inspection of Arms Smoke Helmets.	
6. XI. 15	Patrol & Reconnaissance by 4 Squadrons.	
7. XI. 15	Divisional Headquarters moved to LESTREM.	
8. XI. 15	Church Parade. Inspection of Arms Smoke Helmets. Lecture by O.C on Reconnaissance.	
9. XI. 15 10. XI. 15 11. XI. 15	Squadron worked under Troop arrangements. Map reading. Reconnaissance in Country.	
12. XI. 15 to 17. XI. 15	Squadron worked as General Fatigue making excellent Horse Standings. Shale Rubble foundation with thick Cinder flat on Top.	
17. XI. 15	O.C. rode over to PARADIS (Sheet 36A 1/40,000) Q18.C.8.3) to inspect proposed new Billets.	
18. XI. 15	O.C. rode to Head Qrs. 139th Brigade to arrange about working Party going to trenches. A Fatigue Party worked under C.R.E. at BETHUNE QUAY. Horse Standings completed.	
19. XI. 15	Orders received for Squadron to change Billets to - morrow.	
20. XI. 15	Squadron marched out BETHUNE Billets at 11 am to occupy Billets at Hamel Hill. PARADIS. (reference as above.)	
21. XI. 15	New Billets are very dirty, and every where, and no broken implements had been made whatever by previous Troops in occupation.	

WAR DIARY
or
INTELLIGENCE SUMMARY

(Erase heading not required.)

Army Form C. 2118.

Hour, Date, Place	Summary of Events and Information	Remarks and references to Appendices
22. XI. 15 PARADIS. to 24. XI. 15	Squadron sent party to RICHEBOURG ST VAAST to construct Dug-Outs for 139th Brigade Head Qrs. This party remained up for 3 days and one billeted in RICHEBOURG ST VAAST.	
25. XI. 15	Squadron worked as General Fatigue clearing & improving Billet, making Horse Standings &c.	
26. XI. 15 to 28. XI. 15	Another party proceeded to R.ST.V. for same work and remained until 28th.	
29. XI. 15	Working party at R.ST.V for the day.	
30. XI. 15	ditto	
	On the nights 21st/22nd & 27th/28th they were very hard put to which made it very hard travelling for horses. G.O.C. noticed Billets on 29th & 30th.	

Digby Lawson
Capt.
O.C. "B" Squadron.
Yorkshire Hussars.

46th Div.

"B" Sqn. Yorkshire Hrs.

Date
Vol. XI

WAR DIARY
or
INTELLIGENCE SUMMARY

(Erase heading not required.)

Army Form C. 2118.

Instructions regarding War Diaries and Intelligence Summaries are contained in F. S. Regs., Part II. and the Staff Manual respectively. Title pages will be prepared in manuscript.

Hour, Date, Place		Summary of Events and Information	Remarks and references to Appendices
1 XII 15	PARADIS	Squadron supplied working party for constructing 2nd Oth at RICHEBOURG ST VAAST	
2 XII 15 to	"	} Squadron Routine – Bad floods. Leave cancelled	
4 XII 15	"		
5 XII 15	LA HAYE	Squadron marched out of Billets to new Billets at LA HAYE (1 MILE EAST of ST VENANT).	
6 XII 15 to	"		
9 XII 15	"	Squadron moved under Regular Routine. Being probably under orders to move to the EAST, woollen clothing was drawn in and all deficiencies of equipment made up. G.O.C. inspected Squadron full strength dismounted. Floods rose to 8 inches on road and between Billets. Mules taken in strength to upkeep draught horses.	
10 XII 15	"		
11 XII 15	"	} Squadron Routine. Improving Billets for winter quarters	
12 XII 15 to	"		
18 XII 15	"		
19 XII 15	MONT DE LAMBRES	Squadron marched from LA HAYE to Billets at MONT DE LAMBRES 3 miles SOUTH of AIRE on main road. Billets still occupied by another unit so Men & horses got under cover in LAMBRES for the night.	
20 XII 15	"	Occupied proper Billets – all squadron settled in	
21 XII 15	"	} Squadron Routine. Troop Training. Musketry on 100yd range ended by Squadron on Christmas day. Dinner for Squadron in LAMBRES.	
31st XII 15	"		

Digby Lawson Capt.
B Squadron
for O.C. Yorkshire

D6

"B'h of Yorkshire Hrs
Jan
Vol XI

Army Form C. 2118.

WAR DIARY
or
INTELLIGENCE SUMMARY
(Erase heading not required.)

Instructions regarding War Diaries and Intelligence Summaries are contained in F. S. Regs., Part II. and the Staff Manual respectively. Title pages will be prepared in manuscript.

Hour, Date, Place	Summary of Events and Information	Remarks and references to Appendices
1916.		
1.1.16 to 10.1.16 — MONT DE LAMBRES	Squadron engaged in Troop Training in the fields; also equipped preparatory to moving South. Section a 500 yds. range, and was put through a course of musketry.	During all this period the wind blew very strong from S.W. to N. Squally and showery.
	The stations of Lillers and Bergette were now unfit for training.	
11.1.16 to 13.1.16 — IN THE TRAIN.	The Squadron entrains at LILLERS — departing 9.50 a.m. Halts at ABBEVILLE — ORMOY — MONTEREAU — PIERRELATTE — arrives MARSEILLES 27.m. 13.1.16. Marches 7 miles to CAMP LA VALENTINE.	
13.1.16 to 26.1.16 — CAMP LA VALENTINE MARSEILLE.	The Squadron were under canvas in the large rest camp at this place — where also was The Remount Depôt. The facilities for training in the fields were bad, because the roads for exercising were very restricted — but the Squadron thoroughly cleaned up all Kit and saddlery. Horses were regularly exercised — Instruction given in Musk. Discipline — Foot Drill etc. A number of horses were cast out & others in their place obtained from Remounts. Squadron warned to be ready to embark at short notice. Orders received to entrain for North again at 10.30 a.m. tomorrow.	
27.1.16 to 29.1.16 — 'IN THE TRAIN.'	Squadron paraded 5.30 a.m. Left Camp LA VALENTINE marches to GARE D'ARENC MARSEILLES — entrains — departs 11.30 a.m. Halts at ORANGE — MACON — LES LAUMES — MONTEREAU — CREILL — arrives PONT REMY 2-15 p.m. 29.1.16. Marches 8 kilometres to FAMECHON (1½ K.N.E. AILLY).	
30.1.16 to 31.1.16 — FAMECHON.	Settles into Billets — exercises horses, general clean up after the journey.	

Dafy Jevison Capt
D. Saunders 9
B. Yorkshire 15-2-1-

Army Form C. 2118.

WAR DIARY
or
INTELLIGENCE SUMMARY

(Erase heading not required.)

Instructions regarding War Diaries and Intelligence Summaries are contained in F. S. Regs., Part II. and the Staff Manual respectively. Title pages will be prepared in manuscript.

Hour, Date, Place		Summary of Events and Information	Remarks and references to Appendices
1.2.16 to 11.2.16	FAMECHON	Squadron Training. 1st & 3rd Equitation. 4th Dismounted action. 5th advance guard. 7th to dismounted attack. 8th 10th rearguard action	ref. references LENS 11 / 104,000 A.S.
11.2.16 to 18.2.16	DOM QUEUR	Squadron moved to new Billets at DOM QUEUR. 12th 13th } Squadron Routine. 14th 15th } 6 Reinforcements arrived. advance guard action with establishing 16th Piulins by S.E. & Squadron routine.	" " A.S. bad weather heavy rain. Weather bad.
18.2.16 to 24.2.16	MONT PLAISIR	18th Squadron moved to new Billets at MONTPLAISIR very wet 19th " " 20th Major W.G. Flay, 2/Lt Fairbairn & Beckett went for instruction to 17th Lancers returning 26th 21st Squadron practiced map reading in the field Recruit training 22nd } Gas Helmet Drill 23rd } Gas Attacks	" " D.S. Heavy storm last night
24.2.16 to 29.2.16	CANAPLES	24th Squadron changed Billets to CANAPLES 25th } Squadron routine & dismounted work. 26th } 27th ditto " 28th " "	" " C.6. heavy rain Still frosts & snow
29th	CANDAS	6 Reinforcements arrived. Squadron changed Billets to CANDAS.	" " D.S. D. for O/C B.SQUADRON YORKSHIRE HRS.

13. Squadron
Yorkshire Hrs

WAR DIARY
or
INTELLIGENCE SUMMARY
(Erase heading not required.)

Army Form C. 2118.

10/4/16

Place	Date	Hour	Summary of Events and Information	Remarks and references to Appendices
CANDAS	1/3/16		Squadron settling into Billets – W.O.E. and Dr. to SHQ at DRUILLERS.	
"	2.3.16 to 6		Squadron worked under Troop arrangement. R.S.M. continued instruction of Reinforcements in equitation. Full marching order, in which they are very motivated.	LENS II. 100,000 D.5
	4.3.16		Inspection – dug down on ground.	
	5.3.16		Church Parade with 8th Notts & Derbys.	
ST BIRVILLE	6.3.16		D.L. went on early as Billeting Officer and Squadron paraded 6.30 AM and marched to SIBIVILLE A.P.M. 46th Divn. 1st 908th. Rifles and 17 ORS attached to him as MHP during this move.	LENS 100,000 D 3.
	7.3.16 Co		Squadron worked under Troop arrangement, in ordinary Routine.	
	8.3.16		From the 3rd to 9th inst. This trend to much snow and frost, that it made work on the roads almost impossible, and severely hindered the Squadron Routine.	
GOUY EN TERNOIS	9.3.16		D.L. in advance Billeting officer. Squadron marched in at 12 NOON, much difficulty in billeting owing to congestion of Troops.	LENS E.3.
	10.3.16		Squadron settled in Billets. Lieut D.L. Isept. 611 Men left for C.H.Q. to attend Course of Instruction in Hotchkiss Rifle at Machine Gun School. 3 Men discharged.	
AUBIGNY	11.3.16		Snow still on ground. Squadron changed Billets to AUBIGNY	FRANCE C.51. 40,000
BETHONSART	12.3.16		Thaw set in. Squadron changed Billets to BETHONSART – no return of Officers to all Crept. O.A.M. went to Phelson at VILLERS BRULIN / Military	D 17B
AFF	13.3.16		Squadron settled into Billets, and Cried to clean Village, which was filthy having had been evacuated by French Troops – French flying officer billeted in village killed	FRANCE 36/B 40,000 V.V.1B
	14.3.16		by Aeroplane during a nose dive. Squadron Routine improving Billets	
	15.3.16		G.O.C. Cav. Cps to sept Village officers they came up to BETHONSART to Billet / not received by such flying person.	

B. Squadron
Yorkshire Hussars

WAR DIARY
or
INTELLIGENCE SUMMARY
(Erase heading not required.)

Army Form C. 2118.
2
10.4.16

Place	Date	Hour	Summary of Events and Information	Remarks and references to Appendices
BETHONSART	16.3.16		Rct of Squadron. Inspection by O.C. W.G.E. rode to D.H.Q. about digging party.	FRANCE 36B / 40,000 V 21.B.
	17.3.16		At " " " "	
	18.3.16		Squadron clean up. Inter Troop football match afternoon.	
	19.3.16		N.W.7 ard 20 O.R.s rode to M.T. St Eloy.	
			Officer to BERTHONVAL FARM where they were billeted for the 4 days during which they were working on D.H.Q. advance dug outs.	
	20.3.16		Squadron worked under Troop arrangements. Re Inoculation started against para typhoid. D.H. as party returned from Machine Gun School.	
	21.3.16 to 23.3.16		Squadron Routine, Horse Exercise, Innoculation, Baths etc.	
	23.3.16		N.W.7 returned to Billets.	
	24.3.16		Drop Down as Gaswal - Inspection of Kit etc. clean up.	
	25.3.16		W.G.E. visited Working Party at Trenches. Working party recalled by D.H.Q. the night.	
	26.3.16		Church Parade cancelled owing to wet. Rent officer came & made arrangements	
	27.3.16		D.H. started Hotchkiss Rifle Class for Squadron Instructors. Splm worked under Troop Arrangements	
			W.G.E. went on leave.	
	28.3.16		Squadron Routine. Horse Exercise. Hotchkiss Classes. Demolition Classes etc.	
	29.3.16		do. E.B. evacuated to hospital.	
	30.3.16		G.H.H. & No 1 Troop left for new attachment to 17th the cart. N.W.7 & party proceeded M.T. St Eloy to start new digging work. lived in dug outs. Equitation started over jumps. Treat & breast harness horse cleaned by R.F.M.	

B. SQUADRON YORKSHIRE
Lawson Capt
A/Capt f/ O.C.
B Sqn YORKSHIRE

May 4th 1916.

Army Form C. 2118.

B Squadron
Yorkshire Hrs

WAR DIARY
or
INTELLIGENCE SUMMARY
(Erase heading not required.)

Instructions regarding War Diaries and Intelligence Summaries are contained in F.S. Regs., Part II and the Staff Manual respectively. Title Pages will be prepared in manuscript.

Place	Date	Hour	Summary of Events and Information	Remarks and references to Appendices
BETHONSART	1.4.16.		Squadron Routine - short of men for horses, working party at front. At Eloy	Sheet 36 B V 21 b. 8. 8.
	2.4.16.		Inspection. N.W.F. + party relieves from Mont St. Elly.	
	3.4.16.		Field day under Sir Julian Byng K.O.B. 17th Corps - with 6th (Divisional Cavalry) + North Staffs Horse and Lothians + Border Horse and Divisional Cyclist Coy.	
	4.4.16.		Equitation for Reinforcements. R.S.M.	
			D.L. training Squadron instructors in Hotchkiss rifle.	
	5.4.16.		R.W.B. and party to work on dug-outs Mont St. Eloy.	
			2nd Lt. Napier + 6 O.R.'s of Lothians + Border Horse - 2nd Div. Cav. arrives for 5 days Hotchkiss Rifle Course + were billeted on Squadron.	
			Staff Ride for Officers of Corps. Mts. Troops under G.O.C. Corps.	
	6.4.16.		Sqdn. Routine - Fatigues worked building jumps.	
	7.4.16.		do. Lt. W.F.E. returns from leave.	
	8.4.16.		do.	
	9.4.16.		School Parade with Cyclists. N.W.F. and party relieves R.W.B. and party at digging.	
			G.O.C. 46th Div. inspected our Billets in afternoon.	
	10.4.16.		Equitation for Squadron. Hotchkiss Class returned to Billets. W.F.E. and D.L.	
			visited working party at Mont St. Eloy.	
	11.4.16.		2nd Detachment of Lothians and Border Horse came for 5½ days instructional Hotchkiss	
			Rifle Course + Billeted with on Squadron.	
	12.4.16.		Bad weather continues - exercising only.	
	13.4.16.		Very showery - Equitation. R.W.B. + party relieves N.W.F. + party at Mont St. Eloy.	
	14.4.16.		Showery - Equitation under R.S.M. Squadron pay.	
	15.4.16.		Heavy showers all morning. Further working party of 21 N.C.O's + Men at Divisional School ACNIERES for the day.	

2449 Wt. W14957/M90 750,000 1/16 J.B.C. & A. Forms/C.2118/12.

Continued.

WAR DIARY
or
INTELLIGENCE SUMMARY
(Erase heading not required.)

Army Form C. 2118.

Instructions regarding War Diaries and Intelligence Summaries are contained in F. S. Regs., Part II. and the Staff Manual respectively. Title Pages will be prepared in manuscript.

Place	Date	Hour	Summary of Events and Information	Remarks and references to Appendices
BETHONSART.	16.4.16.		Church Parade with Cyclists. Hotchkiss class returns to Kellek. W.I.L. and remainder of Sqdn. Localities	Sheet 36 B. V.24. 8.8.
	17.4.16.		Equitation cancelled owing to wet. Sqdn. exercises horses. N.W.F. & party relieve R.W.B. & party digging at	C.7.c. but S.I.C. Mont St. Eloy. Fed. 11. 8 shd.
			D.L. went to see progress new Billets at AVERDOIN O.T.	36 B.
	18.4.16.		Rains all day. Sqdn. exercises horses.	
	19.4.16.		Lt. Kirkpatrick and 40 O.R's came for 3 days refresher course on Hotchkiss Rifle. returned to Billets. AVERDOINGT horse lines out.	
			D.L. enters with Major Freedom to see new Billets at TERNAS. Been worked at.	
	20.4.16.		Captain Vivian Lockett 17th Lancers having come to 17th Corps to instruct h/o Troops. arrived 9 a.m.	
			to lecture to Officers & N.C.O's of Squadron. & Divl. Cyclist Co. N.W.F. & party relieved from digging	
			Fatigue party starts taking down jumps preparatory to move.	
	21.4.16.		W.I.L. & D.L. went to inspect Billets at TERNAS.	Sheet 51 C.
			Horse exercise - preparing for move.	B.15.4.5.8.
TERNAS.	22.4.16.		Sqdn. parades 11 a.m. + marches to TERNAS.	
	23.4.16.		Celebration of Holy Communion - Church Parade after - settling into Billets. Football match	Sheet 51 C. C.8.
			Lt. Cheston + 6 O.R's North Irish Horse came for 5½ days Hotchkiss course. Returns to Billets	
	24.4.16.		Field Day for Corps Divl. Mtd Troops under Capt. Lockett - around Bois DES HEROM BUS.	
	25.4.16.		Officers + N.C.O's of Sqdn. attended lecture by Capt. Lockett. Wet morning horses sent out by	
			Sqdn. worked under Troop arrangements. Horses moves from stables to lines afternoon.	
	26.4.16.		Lecture by Capt. Lockett morning. Lecture by Lt. Col. Heine in afternoon.	
	27.4.16.		Sqdn. worked in Field under Troop arrangements. N.I.H. Hotchkiss class arrives.	
	28.4.16.		Lecture by Capt. Lockett + work in field in morning. Lt. Ludlaw + 2nd Detachment of	
	29.4.16.		North Irish Horse came for 5½ days Hotchkiss Rifle Course.	
	30.4.16.		Church Parade with Cyclists. Trial football match with Cyclists to choose team for	
			G.O.C's cup in afternoon.	

2449 Wt. W14957/M90 750,000 1/16 J.B.C.& A. Forms/C.2118/12.

Army Form C. 2118

WAR DIARY
or
INTELLIGENCE SUMMARY
(Erase heading not required.)

B. Squadron.
Yorkshire Hussars.
Divl. Cavalry.
46th Division.

Instructions regarding War Diaries and Intelligence Summaries are contained in F.S. Regs., Part II. and the Staff Manual respectively. Title Pages will be prepared in manuscript.

Place	Date	Hour	Summary of Events and Information	Remarks and references to Appendices
TERNAS	1.5.16		B. Sqdn. Yorks. Hrs. 46 Divl. Cyclist Co. & 2 Coys. M.M.G. worked all day on Bogs. Scheme - Acting on 2nd Lines to a Brigade of Infantry proceeding from Lt. Col. to Bracy. Hotchkiss classes - dismounted swords drill under R.S.M.	Sheet 57.C. Bq. d. 8. 2.
	2.5.16		Squadron work. Sqdn. warned that Division is moving South. 137 Bde. rcd. 1.807.	
	3.5.16		Evolution. Sqdn. ran H.S. Horse finished. Hf. sections. Jumping Competition W. H. J. H. in afternoon. Squadron Hotchkiss class for H.S. Horse finished.	
	4.5.16		Orders to Start fast. When Division moves.	
	5.5.16		Capt. Lockett lectures to N.C.O.s of Squadron & Divl. Cyclist Co. H.Q. 2nd 46th Division came to say goodbye to us on their way South, & told us we were to become Corps Cavalry & that no other two Squadrons would join up with us.	
	6.5.16		D.L. & Bellwind rode Govt. En Ternois before breakfast to look at Billets. Scheme by Capt. Lockett in the field for Officers & N.C.O.s. D.L. & R.H.R. went to Paris to Lane.	B28. d.8.14
	7.5.16		Church Parade. Preparation for move.	
Gouy-En-Ternois	8.5.16		Squadron moves to Gouy. En Ternois. Parade 10 a.m. Letters into Billets. C. Squadron arrives near from 49 Division near AMIENS.	
	9.5.16		Very wet day. Work in Billets.	
	10.5.16		Capt. Lockett lectures afternoon. A. Sqdn. arrives 1.0 p.m. from 50th Division at GODERSVAERVELDE - Regiment together once more. Major Eley acting o/c. till things are settled. H.W.J. doing o/c. B. Squadron and temporary adjutant.	
	11.5.16		W. & C. & L. Lane Troops Lowfield 2 no.	
	12.5.16		Squadron exercise. H. & D. M. G. A. Mills recalled to England to take tractors. Squadron ditte Swords drill & equitation under H. D.M. Bellwind recalls to 46 Division.	C.8.
	13.5.16		Gun Section at Biely. Regimental Field Day round BOIS DES HEROMBUS. Bellwind to 46 Division.	
	14.5.16		Squadron exercise. Mills left for England.	
	15.5.16		Troop lectures. Very wet morning.	

Army Form C. 2118

WAR DIARY
or
INTELLIGENCE SUMMARY
(Erase heading not required.)

Instructions regarding War Diaries and Intelligence Summaries are contained in F. S. Regs., Part II. and the Staff Manual respectively. Title Pages will be prepared in manuscript.

(2)

Place	Date	Hour	Summary of Events and Information	Remarks and references to Appendices
COUP-EN-TERNOIS	16.5.16.		Horses all seen by Veterinary Officer.	
	17.5.16.		Rgt. 1 R.H.B. relieves from Paris. B1 becomes regtal. Left ½ Squadron did sword drill & equitation. Rgt. ½ Squadron Dismounted Action at MONTS-EN-TERNOIS.	B20. L.7.0
	18.5.16.		Squadron sprint horses & baths near SARS, LES. BOIS. (Horses do 9 miles a day have gone to trots & back). 2nd Lt. Morton T.T. arrives to Squadron.	H18. c. 3-3
	19.5.16		Squadron Scheme at MONTS-EN-TERNOIS.	
	20.5.16		Troops went out to reconnoitre road down to Corps Front line. (Very hot day).	
	21.5.16.		Inspection in morning. Football match v English at TERNAS afternoon.	
	22.5.16.		Troop arrangements. R.H.B. has slight attacks of his horse when at gallop.	
	23.5.16.		Squadron dismounted parade in morning. Squadron Sports 5.30 p.m.	
	24.5.16.		Regtl. Parade in A.M. on MAIZIÈRES Rd. Mtr. to practise Mounted Party for advance into Corps scheme. Hotchkiss Gun started. M.S.E. had staff for Officers & sergeants.	B10. L. 4.8
	25.5.16		Bt. 7.R.W.7. & C.E. & L.7. wrote 4 Corps. & Imp. Indian Lechers afternoon W.S.E. & L.7. note 4 Corps & Imp. Indian Lechers	
	26.5.16.		Sword Drill for N.C.O's in morning. Bt. 7.R.W.7. note to Corps. Wires that Major Orpen was coming to take command of Regiment. Afternoon Dismounted Parade to practise tactics over Fanchee.	
	27.5.16.		Transport inspection by Bt. in morning. Regimental Dismounted Sports after tea. Col. Diary Keepl. & Officers 17th Lancers came over to tea.	
	28.5.16.		Church Parade morning. Corps Commander Sir Charles Ferguson came in afternoon.	
	29.5.16.		Sqdn. did dismounted Action in morning. Saddle inspection afternoon - Mr. with Hotchkiss Guns on Range all morning.	C.5. a. 00
	30.5.16.		Squadron parades dismounted for bayonet drill A.M. Heavy Rain. Bath. TINCQUES afternoon. 2nd Lt. L.E. Orville arrives as reinforcement to Squadron. went to see 17th Lancers defence of village.	
	31.5.16.		Horses selected for show in A.M. D.D.R. 3rd Army came to cast horses. Wire to say that Major Orpen has left ETAPLES.	R.R.7. E.Y.

Sidley Dawson Cpt.
for O.C. B Squadron
(Yorkshire H.)

1875 Wt. W593/826 1,000,000 4/15 J.B.C. & A. A.D.S.S./Forms/C. 2118.

www.ingramcontent.com/pod-product-compliance
Lightning Source LLC
Chambersburg PA
CBHW081248170426
43191CB00037B/2081